Boc



An Author's Guide

# Rob Watts

Ocean View Press • Boston

# Book Signing 101: An Author's Guide

## The Do's, Don'ts and Expectations Involved in Professional Book Signing

Book Signing 101: An Author's Guide (The Do's, Don'ts and Expectations Involved in Professional Book Signings)



ISBN: 978-0-9761916-1-2

Second Edition

Watts, Rob

Book Signing 101: An Author's Guide / Rob Watts. – Second Edition

RobWattsOnline.com

## Introduction

This book is about a subject in which I have gained some insight over the years---professional book signing. My journey started in a way that I'm sure most of yours had; I wrote a book, published it, and then wondered how in the world I was going to get my book in the hands of readers. Prior to starting on my own path to writing a book, I had attended many book signings of authors whom I held in high regard. I watched as fans eagerly awaited their turn to meet the author with books in hand, elated and excited to meet their hero and get their signature planted on their published work. The authors had handlers fetching them beverages, while bookstore staff kept the constant flow of fans organized in line while the level of excitement seemed to escalate by the minute. How incredible---it must be like this for all authors who write books; or so I thought.

There's a terrific scene in the 2011 film, *Twixt,* in which novelist Hall Baltimore (played by Val Kilmer) drives around a one-horse town in search of the local bookstore that's hosting his book signing. To his disappointment, it's revealed that the "bookstore" is in-fact the local hardware store with a book shelf at the front of the establishment. Don't fool yourself; no matter how well an author's book may be selling, or no matter how much praise it's receiving in professional trades and on Amazon; mark my words, there isn't an author out there who hasn't shown up to their own book signing in such Spartan conditions at least once in their career.

While I’ve been fortunate enough to have some of my book signings held in cozy bookstores, there have been many times where I’ve sold books at rundown shopping malls, in the rain at outdoor venues, in a freezing cold sports arena, empty VFW halls in the middle of nowhere and a comic con where I was placed next to a belly dancer who danced with a snake every fifteen minutes. Ah, the glitz and glamour of an independent author.

As independent authors---traditionally published authors included---we feel a sense of validation for our hard work when we're able to present our books to a public audience. Although it's not necessary that we take our books on the road---many would argue that social media is a more effective and viable marketing tool--- it still offers us a sense of pride and accomplishment when we have physical proof of our accomplishments displayed before us. We like to feel special; we like to feel appreciated---even if it's for a few short hours, we want our moment in the spotlight to be worth its weight in gold. How well we shine in that spotlight is primarily up to us, though.

Like any successful endeavor in life, one thing's for certain, it's always achieved by working hard and staying focused. With success, you only get back what you're willing to put in, and the business of successful book signings is no exception. You are doing yourself a harsh injustice by simply allowing your books---books that you've spent countless and tedious hours writing---to die on the vine by not properly promoting them. You simply can't just sit back and depend on a few positive reviews on Amazon and some word of mouth from your writer friends on Facebook to sell your book for you. Putting yourself and your book in front of the book buying public, fellow authors and event coordinators is what will make your efforts worthwhile.

Like many of you reading this, I, at one time, had no idea how to coordinate a book signing. I probably had the same questions that many of you have. Who am I supposed to contact? Do I need to bring my own folding table and chairs? How many books do I have to have with me? Where should I hold a book signing? How far away should I hold a book signing? What if nobody shows up? What do I do if people actually show up? Is a bookstore the only place to hold a book signing? So on and so forth. These are just a handful of questions that I wound up answering though trial and error over the years while promoting my books. While there is no one-size-fits-all method to book promotion, one thing can be agreed upon and that is that what works for one person might not work for another. It takes time and effort to discover what will work best for you. Once you find your ideal venue and get your rhythm, there will be no stopping you.

While I don't claim to be a certified expert on the topic of book signings and book promotion, I do have a number of years of experience behind me and I can tell you this; you'll have successful book selling days and some bad ones. You'll meet some wonderful new friends at some events and not so much at others. You'll make beneficial contacts that might propel you to the next level at some events and meet some negative minded individuals at some others. Good days and bad days happen and professional book events are certainly no exception. Your success depends on you being armed with a positive can-do attitude. Be prepared for anything and everything. Just remember that at the end of the day, your objective is to sell books, make a good impression on your future fans and network with people who can introduce you to future event opportunities. If you achieve all three in one day, you've hit the jackpot.

Hopefully, you'll find the following pieces of advice beneficial to you as you begin your journey into the world of professional book signing.

# 1: Where should you hold book signings?

## The Large Bookstore Chains

It's understandable that an author who's looking to branch out with their literary work would want to start right at the top of the bookseller food chain by signing books at Barnes and Nobel or Books-a-Million. I will tell you right now that it's not the simplest of tasks obtaining a spot on the much coveted events calendar at either one of these book seller giants. There are many hurdles and gatekeepers to pass before you get to secure your spot on their roster. Although ambitious and toilsome, it's not entirely impossible to achieve.

The one thing you need to remember is, in most cases, big book chains such as B&N and Books-a-Million tend to host bestselling authors who undoubtedly are going to draw a large book buying crowd. Barnes and Nobel, for instance, hosts more than 28,000 author events across the United States each year. These author events are typically organized and financed by the authors' publisher. If you're up to the challenge, here is what you'll need prior to contacting the events coordinator, community relations manager or general manager to the location you'd like to have your event.

- A professionally published book; a book that has been professionally edited, has a registered ISBN number, has a professionally designed cover and isn't published by a print-on-demand (POD) service.

- Have a brief synopsis of your book memorized and ready to go. This is your elevator pitch. You might correspond via email with an events coordinator but you might speak to them on the phone or in person and you're going to want to have your entire book's pertinent information ready to fire off. The same can be said for your ISBN number. The coordinator is going to want this information and if you can't provide it or your book isn't registered with an ISBN number; you can count on any consideration of a book signing to be off of the table.
- A convincing pitch as to why you and your book would be of interest to its customers.

Notice I used the phrase, "its customers." Keep in mind that you'll be a guest in their establishment and they are in-fact allowing you access to their patrons during the course of your time in the store. You might have a dedicated fan base, and you'll be expected to draw them into the store as well (read on), but as far as the store is concerned, they want reassurance that everyday regular customers will purchase your book in addition to what they walked in there for. If they believe that another author looking to fill a book signing slot in their store will be a better draw, they are going with that other author.

**Local Independent Bookstores**

These are venues that you should highly consider; especially if your story takes place in a certain local community. Look into setting up a signing in that town or community. Some, not all, but some independently-owned bookstores will be happy to host your signing, provided you offer them some perks in return. Such as, you'll be expected to heavily promote the signing and the bookstore. You'll be expected to provide the store with books; books that you will sell to them at wholesale price, which they will sell through their store and pay you your portion of sales after they have deducted their cost.

It's also important to point out that it's not as simple as calling up the store and asking if you can host a book signing in their store. Although Indie bookstores like to wave the "we support indie and local authors" flag, it's still a very parochial community and if you're an unknown author who has never set foot in their store, gotten to know the owners or manager, or even spent money in their store, they are most likely going to refuse your request. It's a, *you scratch my back and I'll scratch yours* type of game. Stop into a few of these stores on a regular basis. Get to know the owner or manager, and more importantly, get them to know you. This will help in getting a signing hosted down the line.

**Author Conventions & Expos**

These types of events are great for networking and meeting fellow authors. They're sometimes not so great for book sales, because you are after all, competing with a room full of other authors---authors who are trying to sell *their own* books. But, I am a big fan of these types of venues because sometimes meeting the right people at an event is far more valuable than a few extra book sales. While there are plenty of genre-specific author expos out there throughout the United States, don't hesitate to branch out of your comfort zone. Multi-genre author events are a terrific way to expand your horizons and your professional network.

## Comic Cons

Unless you're an author of a graphic novel or comic book—or some kind of illustrated book, then you probably won't do very well at these. Booking table space at a comic con is pricey---upwards of $150.00 to $400.00, for a two or three day event. It's costly and unless you sell enough books to at least make the cost of your table back, it's simply not good business. Sometimes it's more feasible to share the cost of a table with another author, but again, the cost still adds up. In addition to your table fee, you need to consider food; lodging, gas—it can really add up and you'll hardly ever make your investment back in book sales. Plus, are you up for sitting behind your table from 10am to 6pm on both a

Saturday and Sunday? Your time might be better spent doing something else.

The other thing to consider when thinking about signing at a comic con is that (and this is based on personal experience) most comic con attendees don't care about literary books. This isn't meant to be an insult. After all, if you were attending a BBQ food festival, would you care about someone serving tofu? Perhaps a few of you might, but most of you would not. Comic con attendees are primarily there to dress up in costume, buy comics, toys, action figures, meet celebrities and so on. The admission fees for these events aren't cheap either---upwards of forty dollars per person at certain events.

Celebrity autographs and pictures are also taxing on the old wallet, as celebrity figures charge anywhere from twenty to eighty dollars. Once kids, and/or their parents have spent a large sum of money on all this stuff, books from an unknown author aren't very high on their list of priorities. I've done these events, they are fun, I've done okay in sales at one or two of them, but I hate to say, most have been a big waste of time and money.

To put this in perspective; I once spent two days behind a table at a local comic con / horror con, and the attendance for Saturday alone was an astounding 20,000 attendees. Sunday was almost as impressive with close to 12,000 attendees. 32,000 people walking by my table over the course of two days and do you want to take a guess at how many books I sold that weekend? Five---five books at a cost of $20.00 per book, earning me $100.00 in book sales. I didn't come close to covering the cost of my table and any other expenses that I had that weekend. We'll touch on this subject in greater detail further along.

## Arts and Craft Fairs

Depending on the location of the event, you could have successful book sales. I've done these types of events in the past and I've done rather well. *Well,* meaning I sold a few books, which were enough to cover my table cost and the gas that it took to drive there. Sometimes though, I've done poorly, and left with my financial book in the red for that afternoon. It's also worth mentioning that a lot of craft fairs are held in local church halls. I can tell you from first-hand experience that writers, say in the horror genre, are perceived as Satan worshipers by many craft fair goers. The mere mention that you're a horror writer is enough to scare them off to the other side of the room. They make you feel as welcomed as a drag queen at a monster truck rally.

The good news is these events are low cost. Sometimes table space cost as little as $20-40 dollars for an afternoon. Usually, you will be the only author selling books. That's your leverage. Keep in mind that most people who come out to these events aren't expecting to buy books by unknown authors. Their first impression as they walk over to your table of books will be that you are simply selling books. They won't realize that *you* are the author. Be sure to engage with them quickly and get them interested in the titles you, the author, are selling.

Experiment at a few of these events. Only you know the subject matter of the books you are selling, and you alone know what type of personality you have that will attract a book buying audience. See what works well for you and make notes for the future. Once you find what works in your favor, stay on that path.

**Coffee Shops**

Books and coffee go together like apple pie and ice cream so it makes sense to approach some local mom and pop coffee houses about hosting your book signing. You'd be surprised at just how many small coffee establishments will be open to the idea. The best part is that it won't cost you anything to be there. Your only investment will be your time, your books and your marketing materials---which you should already have on hand and ready to go. Local coffee houses often have a cozy charm about them that lends well to a book signing setting. Honestly, I'm baffled as to why these establishments aren't utilizing their space for local artists more often these days.

**Public Libraries**

These are the venues where you'll feel right at home holding book signings. There's no greater setting than an institution that caters to the pursuit of knowledge by making available an endless supply of resources that educate, entertain and stimulate our mind. By encouraging your fans to attend events at public libraries, you're doing these institutions a great service, simply by getting the public to enter through the doors.

Call a few of your local libraries and ask to speak with the program/events coordinator. Introduce yourself and inform them that you're an author interested in setting up a book signing/reading at their branch. Be prepared to pitch your book's synopsis, the genre and any pertinent information that will convince the library that you'd be a good candidate for an appearance.

# 2: What you will need to have with you at your book signings

**Books**

I know this probably seems painfully obvious, but if you don't have a good supply of your books with you, you won't have a good book signing. Depending on where your signing is taking place, it's important to have a reasonable amount of stock available for sale. I would suggest anywhere between fifteen to thirty copies of the book that you're promoting. Sometimes a bookstore will have your books in stock at their location, but more than likely, you will be signing in a location where you'll be responsible for your own supply of books, so, have a good supply of them. This doesn't mean that every book will be sold; it means that you're covering yourself from the embarrassment of running out of your stock and missing out on a book sale.

**Tablecloth**

Occasionally, tablecloths will be provided for you at a signing event; however, more-often-than-not you'll be bringing your own. Your table will look bare and unprofessional otherwise. The color and material of your tablecloth is entirely up to your discretion. There really is no right or wrong color when it comes to the way you wish to promote your work. Perhaps your latest book cover is blue and you wish to make that color your focal point; maybe you want to keep it simple with a bright white or maybe a stark black. Do what compliments your book best.

Tablecloths are easy to find and inexpensive to purchase. The least expensive are the disposable plastic variety and can be purchase for a few dollars at your local party supply store.

**Marketing Materials**

Marketing materials are a must for independent authors. These are items that you have to be willing to spend money on in order to give them away for free. What you purchase and how much you spend on items---ones that will generate sales for your book, is entirely up to you. Start off with some low-risk, low-cost promo items such as bookmarks, postcards and business cards; anything that bares your book cover or author info and can easily be handed out. These items are affordable and available through places like Vista Print.

Signs and table banners are also useful and eye catching but sometimes they're unnecessary. You don't always need awkward and oversized pop up signage at every event that you do. These things can be a hassle depending upon where in the room you are set up. If you're in a confined area, more-often-than-not, people are constantly knocking the signs over as they are walking by. If it's not really practical for your events, don't invest in one. Not right away anyway. My suggestion is make certain that book signing is something that you want to continually do. There's no sense in investing money on promotional items that are only going to wind up in the corner of your garage or basement after one or two attempts on the book signing circuit.

If you decide that you are going to make book promotions your priority and you plan to do five or more events a year, then by all means, get a good quality pop-up sign produced and display it at your table. Make certain that you use a high-quality image on the banner, otherwise it will look pixilated and poorly-produced. You don't want to waste your money on a banner that looks unprofessional. I recommend having a professional photographer take photos of you for promotional use---your website, social media, business cards, and of course your pop-up sign. Don't simply scroll through the photos on your Facebook profile until you find one that you think looks good. You want to project professionalism; you want to make a lasting impression. It's worth the cost of a photographer who'll know how to make you look your absolute best.

You'll want to avoid using an image of your book, because if you release multiple books within a short time from one another, your sign will become outdated, forcing you to spend money on a new one. Your professional author photo will serve you better in the long-run. After all, you're selling *yourself* to potential book buyers---hopefully the book sales follow. Be sure to have your name (of course) and website clearly printed on the sign. You may also want to describe yourself further by adding *author of suspense* or *romance writer* to better sell yourself and your work. When all is said and done, however, your best advertisement should be your approachable and engaging presence, and your books in front of you. That's really it.

## An Appropriate form of Dress

Dress professionally and look approachable. Unless it's a themed event, such as a comic con where everyone is walking around in costume, then perhaps it's a fun idea to blend in a bit and join in on the fun with attendees---wearing something along the lines of a superhero shirt or television series.

Wearing a full-fledged costume, head to toe, is not a good idea. For one thing it's uncomfortable after several hours behind a table. Most importantly, if someone is interested in buying your book, you'll want them to see who you are and what you (the author) look like. Unless the picture on the back cover of your book shows you in skull face, leave the costume at home. After all, are you there to sell books or to take part in cosplay?

If you're appearing at a book store, author convention or most any other professional event, look as though you are interviewing for a job position; essentially you are. You're there to gain new fans and book buyers. Just because you're a writer in the genre of horror, don't wear a sloppy looking, blood splattered, horror themed tee-shirt. Believe it or not, only a small margin of people that'll roam past your table will truly *get* what your tee-shirt means. Most won't and possibly could be offended. I'm not suggesting that you dress up in a three-piece suit, but dress nice, wear something that's comfortable on you, show some professionalism and look like an author who's serious about their craft.

**Courtesy**

Unless you're of a certain age or you have a handicap that prevents you from doing so, always stand up when someone approaches you and your table. This is another pet peeve of mine. I can't stand it when I approach an author and they just sit there in their chair, forcing me (a potential book buyer) to lean down in order to speak to the person behind the table. It's very rude and Ill-mannered and it shows a low regard for the person who was gracious enough to visit your table. Don't be just another selfish individual in the world. Speak to your future fan(s) at eye level and don't make them uncomfortable by having to lean in to hear what you're saying. This could be the difference between a book sale and no book sale. I'm not suggesting that you pop up like a carnival funhouse clown every time someone approaches your table. You don't want to appear intimidating or forceful in your sales approach; once someone begins speaking to you, however, stand up and have a friendly and engaging conversation. Appear to enjoy the fact that someone has bothered to visit your table and speak with you. You'll appear all the more professional.

It's also important to keep questionable topics of conversation (politics, religion, sex, etc...) away from your table. Everyone is entitled to have whatever conversation they choose with their friends, but this is not the time or place to engage in a conversation that may be overheard by a potential book buyer who may be insulted or offended. I've personally witnessed such a thing and unfortunately, word got back to the event coordinator and the individual was never invited back to the event again. It's best just to avoid using foul language and discussing sensitive topics within ear reach from your public.

### Pens and Markers

Again, it seems as though I'm stating the obvious, but oftentimes an author will be sitting around for half the day waiting for an interested book buyer, and then boom---someone wants to buy a book, but the author's failed to realize they hadn't brought along anything to sign with. Keep an abundance of writing material with you, especially in the chance that someone will walk away with your pen or marker. It almost always happens.

You'll want to have a variety of quality pens, and depending upon the paper stock of your books, you'll want to make sure you're using the right pen so you won't cause smudging after you sign your name. Here are a few suggestions based on personal experience.

- Zebra Sarasa Push Clip Gel Pens- This is the pen you'll want to use if you don't want to shell out a lot of money. They cost about $2.00 and come in a variety of colored inks---I suggest black ink, however, as it stands out better than blue ink when written on white or off-white paper. If you're signing your name on standard paper, rest assured that the ink from this pen will not smudge.

- Pilot Metropolitan Fountain Pens- When you want to look a tad more professional without breaking the bank, this is a great pen to keep with you at all times, not just at book signings. Priced in the $15.00 range, this brand too comes in a variety of colors and will not smudge when writing on standard paper stock.
- Sharpie- I don't think there's a home in America that doesn't have a Sharpie marker kicking around in a desk drawer. Sharpies are terrific markers and they are great to have on hand at book signings, however, they shouldn't be used to sign your books if you have books that contain standard paper stock. The ink

will bleed right through the page(s) of your book, rendering it damaged. Sharpies or any other colored markers should only be used on books that use heavy coated stock or glossy paper (photo books, cook books, graphic novels.)

**Cash and Credit Card Reader**

Most times, you will be handling the sales of your books right at your table. Unless you're doing an in-store appearance at a large book retailer such as Barnes and Noble who will be handling your sales through their register, be prepared to take money and make change. Also, have a credit card reader with you as well. This will advance your chance of sales if people would rather use their card instead of cash. You don't need the old fashioned knuckle busters anymore. You can get a reader through Intuit or Google Square that plugs directly into your smart phone. Nowadays, the technology allows you to just scan a picture of the card with your camera and it takes the payment; simple as that.

**Hand Sanitizer**

Protect yourself and the people you meet from germs. There potentially could be lots of hand shaking and if you have been handling cash (a well-known germ carrier) then you'd be smart to use your sanitizer regularly.

**Book Stands**

You'll want to display your books upright to give them better visibility. If you don't own them already, you'll want to purchase some folding wire display stands. These can be purchased at arts and crafts outlets such as *Michaels, Hobby Lobby* or online at Amazon---a twelve pack can be purchase for less than twenty dollars---and they travel nicely with the rest of your book signing supplies without taking up too much space.

**Guestbook / Mailing List**

This is a good thing to have on your table, faced out so your potential fans can reach for it easily and jot their name and email down. Keep a pen with your mailing list so they won't need to fish around for something to write with. Whether or not someone buys a book from you, ask if they wouldn't mind signing up for your mailing list. Assure them that you only send out a minimum amount of emails during the year and that they can unsubscribe anytime. I for one shy away from adding my name to an email list due to fear of spam and excessive emails from certain parties. The few lists that I'm on, however, have been very informative and I receive only a few throughout the year. If you're going to send an email newsletter to people who've added their email to your mailing list, it's best to limit your announcements to no more than four a year.

If someone wishes not to add their email to your guestbook, that's okay; simply smile, tell them that you understand and wish them a nice day. You won't get everyone to sign it, but you will get a fair share, and, overtime, you'll be on your way to building an impressive fan base to connect with.

**Pop-Up Canopy Tent (optional)**

The opportunity to do outdoor events may present itself along the way and you'll want to have a pop-up tent to do so. Most organizers of outdoor events require venders to have a canopy tent as part of their display. It keeps the event space uniform and organized and for the benefit of the vender, it shields the sun (or rain) and offers protection to your wares over extended hours throughout the day. Typically, the type of tent you'll need for outdoor events will cost you just north or south of one hundred dollars. You can purchase one at a local outdoor living type of store or one can be easily purchased on Amazon. You'll want either a white or blue canopy (these are widely accepted color schemes at outdoor events), 10 x 10 in size with a cathedral style roof. Most tents include a wheeling storage bag for easy transport. Be sure that it includes stakes to anchor your tent to the ground.

**Emergency Kit**

You never know when a problem could arise and you'll want to be prepared---for safety sake and the sake of your book signing display, so be sure to have the following items on hand.

- Duct Tape- You may need to repair a damaged banner, secure a sign so it doesn't blow away, hold your table cloth down; there are several reasons to keep duct tape on hand---too many to list here, but trust me and keep it with you.
- String- You can use this item for the reasons mentioned above as well as properly

hanging your banners, repairs, so on and so forth.

- Scissors- You may need to cut something on the fly.
- Index Cards- Good to have on hand. You may want to write things down over the course of the day and large index cards don't go missing as easily as Post-Its or notebook paper.
- Band Aids- You or someone nearby may get cut and you'll want to take care of it very quickly, especially before your items fall victim to someone's wound.
- Smart Phone Charger- More than likely, you'll be browsing on your smart phone during your downtime. This eats up your battery; especially if

you're in a bad cell area (lots of venues have poor cell/internet reception.) It's a good idea to have a backup power pack for your charging needs, especially if you're using your smart phone to conduct credit card transactions.

**Additional items to have with you**

- Bottled water or other beverages (non alcohol)
- Light Snacks
- Breath Mints
- Eye Drops
- Sunscreen (if doing outdoor events)

These items are for you, not the public. You could be sitting at a table anywhere from 2-8 hours. You might not have the luxury of getting up and leaving your table unattended. Keep yourself hydrated and fed with light snacks (crackers, candy, small veggies, etc...) Don't bring a full meal. You don't want to have a mouth full of salad or a tuna fish sandwich when a potential book buyer suddenly approaches you. And needless to say, keep wet naps with you to clean your hands after eating anything.

# 3: Things not to bring to your book signings

**Useless Tchotchkes (trinkets)**

As previously mentioned, effective promotional material such as bookmarks and business cards are a good thing to place on your table for people to take away with them. What you don't want to give away are useless trinkets that will never result in anyone paying your website a visit after they've left your sight.

What you SHOULD'NT hand out for free:

- Pens- Everyone loves free pens. We use them every day in life and we can't have enough of them within reach at any one time. Everyone who walks by your table will definitely take a free pen or three. You won't even need to worry about packing them back into your car at the end of the day because they'll be gone. They are, however, not a good investment, and even if they have your website printed on the side, nobody is going to bother to visit your website---okay, perhaps a small percentage will, but it's not very likely that they will purchase one of your books.

- Key chains- Usually, we never really give much thought about key chains. It's something we pick up multiple times a day because we need to start our cars, get into our offices, and lock and unlock our homes. Key chains, however, do have some form of sentimental meaning for us even if we aren't giving it much thought throughout our day. Key chains are usually a form of personality or a special memory. They are given to us as gifts, and we think about and cherish the people who give them to us. Perhaps a key chain is purchased on vacation and it reminds the holder of a fun and less stressful period. They remind us of romantic relationships, family and friends. There is a lot more meaning attached to them than we give credit. With that being said, while it's likely that someone might walk away with a free key chain, it's not very likely that that person will replace their key chain of personal significance with one that has a book cover and website on it. Unless that person is a mega super fan of yours, you'll find that it is money not very well spent.

- Stuffed Animals- Unless it has some sort of significance in your story and it's being used as a tie-in, or you're signing books at multiple children's themed events, then don't invest money in personalized stuffed animals. Although they may dress up your table display and catch an eye or two, people who are attending a book signing or a large author event are there to purchase books. Most grown adults don't want one more thing to bring into their house that they weren't looking for in the first place.

- Food or Candy- Under no circumstances should you make food available at your book signing table. First of all, there are ordinances against handing out free food at public events. You could potentially make yourself (and the venue hosting you) liable in a food poisoning case. Candy bowls is another pet peeve of mine. Don't put a bowl of free candy out on your book table. This only invites people to your table to grab a handful of Snickers bars and walk away. THOSE PEOPLE NEVER SEEM TO BUY ANYTHING. You don't want that type of person at your table, potentially distracting you from someone who might buy your book. Plus, you don't want someone standing in front of your table, stuffing chocolate in their mouth, and then thumbing through your books with chocolate fingers, only to walk away a few minutes later without buying anything anyway. Does J.K. Rowling, Stephen King or Ruta Sepetys place free candy on their table during their book signings? The answer is no and you shouldn't either.

- Free Short Stories (that you've printed from your home computer) - I've seen this on more than one occasion where a possible book buyer approaches the table and before that person has a chance to set eyes on books that are available for purchase, the author waves a bunch of papers stapled together in that person's face and asks, "Would you like a free short story?" There are a couple of things wrong with engaging in this practice.

First of all, handing away free stories looks unprofessional and it screams desperation. It implies that the author has little confidence in his or her own work that's actually *for sale* in front of the customer. Secondly; if you are in-fact hell-bent on handing out a free short story, at least spend a few bucks to run off a semi-professional looking chap book which will be properly bound.

You don’t want to hand someone something that looks like an advertisement for a 50% off mattress sale, because it will end up in the same place where people put their junk mail. And don’t just give your work away for free. If you must offer something, think about giving away the first chapter to your upcoming novel as a way of enticing them into buying it when it’s released. But only give it away to people who buy the book that you’re selling on that day.

## The intimidating friend or family member

This statement might make me very unpopular but I'm going to say it anyway. Leave your unhappy looking and unfriendly friends and family members at home. Although it's a good idea to have a good friend or relative helping you out at your event—to assist with sales or to watch your table while you go to the restroom, it's imperative to have someone with you who gives off the same professional vibe as you. So, with that being said, the wacky cousin who sat in the back of the station wagon on the way to family vacations years ago—leave him at home. The friend who looks as though a potential book buyer is intruding on their personal space?

Leave him or her at home. I know, I know—once we get to know them, we'll see that they are really just big teddy bears on the inside. The problem is, a potential book buyer (aka future fan) has no idea and won't have time to get to know the person who is giving off an intimidating vibe at your table. You have a split second to rope in a book buyer. Don't lose the opportunity by misrepresenting yourself to the general public. I've seen this more than a few times, and although it's unfortunate, it's just a simple fact of today's world. If your friends or family members can't control their loud and abrasive behavior, keep their language clean and not look at strangers approaching your table as if they are ready to throw a punch their way because they are getting too close, don't bring them, plain and simple.

**Hokey Gimmicks**

Again, you're attempting to sell your books while presenting yourself as a professional author---one who esteems the reputation as such. On more than a few occasions, I've seen various attempts to reign in potential customers by inviting them to win a prize by spinning a wheel, playing hangman, picking a card; any card, and tossing a sponge ball into a hole in a cardboard box. Look, if you feel that your table should resemble something from a travelling carnival or the set of the game show *The Price is Right*, that's entirely up to you. Bear in mind that you'll need to lug these unnecessary props around with the rest of your book signing items---your essential items. The other attraction getters won't really help you sell more books; they'll only make you look like a desperate author who has no confidence in your book's own merit.

### What You SHOULD Hand Out For Free

In the previous section, I made note of items that you should avoid handing out for free at your signing events. The following is a list of items that I highly recommend handing out to anyone who approaches your table, whether they purchase a book or not.

- Professional looking business cards. Make sure that it

contains the following important information: Your name, your email address, your website and your most used social media destinations. Keep the design clean and simple to read. Don't clutter it with too much information. You could include a photo of yourself on the card as long as it's a professional looking photo and it doesn't take up too much space on the card. Keep it contained to the top left corner if possible. Heavier stock cards with a gloss coating will cost a little more money, but in the long-run, it will be worth the extra cost. People tend to keep quality looking (and feeling) business cards over the cheaper flimsy ones. The amount of cards you order is entirely up to you. If you know you'll be doing a continual string of signings into the foreseeable future, you may want to order 250-500. I wouldn't recommend buying more than that, though. I also don't recommend including your current book cover on the card. It's possible that you could release a new book (or more) before you've depleted your current stock of business cards, making them appear outdated before their time.

- Bookmarks- People love free bookmarks and they will use

them. You can design custom bookmarks online using (whichever company you search out online) their free online design tools, just be sure that your name and website is legible in large font along both sides of the bookmark.

- Stress Balls- I know it sounds weird but they do make great giveaways. Unfortunately, we are living in stressful times full of safety risks and financial uncertainty. People use stress balls at their office, at home, in their car---just about anywhere. I use them and they do relieve stress. Again, you can search online and find companies who will personalize your item and offer them for a decent price. Make sure your name and website are printed on them. That's all you'll need. They are an inexpensive giveaway and they won't get thrown away. The potential that your website will get a visit from a stress ball is far greater than it would from a free pen.

# 4: Signing alone or with other authors

Occasionally authors like to team up with other authors and share table rental space as a cost cutting measure---events such as comic cons can be extremely pricey, and sometimes a group of authors from writing groups will share a table for the same benefit. Based on my own experience, I am going to say go it alone or with one other author who you work well with in a small space and for long periods of time during an event. Unfortunately, I can count the amount of authors whom I feel comfortable sharing a table with on one hand with fingers left to spare. Mass author signings (3-7 or even more authors at a table or booth) is a very bad idea. First of all, it's much too crowded behind an eight foot table. It's intimidating for a potential book buyer who approaches a booth with multiple sets of eyes on them, pressuring them into to buying their book over another author's. And someone walking over to the booth doesn't want to be put in the position of disappointing anyone by buying one person's book over another. I know I wouldn't.

I find that I just can't be myself behind a table filled with numerous people. I myself am not a Type A personality. I'm not a shrinking violet either, but I'm not the type of person who jumps right up in front of a potential book buyer like a carnival barker in a desperate attempt to make them buy my book. And I don't want to feel like a contestant on Jeopardy—where if I don't hit the buzzer fast enough, I'm locked out of the round.

If someone approaches me or my books, I will say hello, let them know I'm available to answer any questions about my books and then I back off. If my books are enticing enough to them to ask me about them, I will gladly talk their ear off. If it's not their cup of tea, that's fine. My books aren't for everyone. But I'll never be that type of person who desperately rides someone until they are pressured into buying my book. It's very tacky in my honest opinion. The bottom line is, when a large group of authors are selling books at the same table, it's only natural that *everyone* wants to sell books. Sometimes, not always, but sometimes other authors will step in front of you or your book (known as book blocking) and desperately try to sell their book over yours instead. From my experiences at these types of signings, it's just not good business. It also leaves behind resentment and bad blood among your fellow writers.

Plus, with all of those various personalities lingering about, there are certain folks that will have their own ideas on how to better sell books, oftentimes leaving you frustrated and dumbfounded. I myself don't want to sit behind a cluttered table with anything other than my own books in front of me. So, when I know of authors who like to place their stuffed animals with their website on them all over the table, bowls of candy, and their free novellas printed off their home computer, or when people act like used car salesmen—I tend to decline my time and efforts at these events.

I do have a select few authors in my circle who I'm delighted to share book signing space with. I almost always jump at the chance to work with them at the event because they share my philosophy and they're fun to spend the day with, but usually it's best and more effective to go it alone.

# 5: How far away should you hold a book signing?

As far as you'd like, after all, you're trying to build a large audience so don't limit yourself. However, don't start on the other side of the country. Do some small signings in your local community. Build your audience regionally and work outward. Don't break the bank in travel expenses unless it's absolutely beneficial to you. It's important to factor in all the costs involved in a destination signing. If it's in another state, make sure you factor in fuel, lodging, food, emergency cash, et cetera. If you are lodging for the event, make sure you know the distance between your hotel and the venue prior to your trip. It's possible that a miscommunication could happen, and when your signing is in downtown Toronto, you could be lodging an hour away in Etobicoke,

Ontario (yes, it's happened to me.) In the case of my overseas signings, I had set them up prior to my arrival to coincide with my vacation. It killed two birds with one stone. Usually, I limit my book tour traveling to New England and the Tri-State area.

# 6 : Successfully promoting your event

There are several steps an author can take to promote a signing event. The following list of suggestions are highly critical and most effective in getting the word out.

- Create a Facebook Event Page announcing the event. Add an attractive photo, give specific details about the event such as the date and time, the address and anything else that you'll want attendees to know. Make it easy for your fans to find the location of the venue ; if the address is simply 2756 Route 46, that's not very encouraging. Do a quick map search and find some landmarks to point out to your fans. If the venue is located next door to a Burger

King, a gas station or any other easily identifiable landmark, let them know. If there is free parking, let them know that as well. The more details you offer, the more appealing your event will be to fans. Once your page is written and spell checked, send it out to all of your friends, even the ones who don't live anywhere near the book signing event. Even if they don't live near you or the event location, they will be made aware of your event and the fact that you have a book available for sale. This increases your book's visibility and sales potential.

- Write a blog post and include everything you've written in your Facebook Event Page. Add any additional photos or links that will better serve your event's potential success.

- Post about it on Twitter. Share the link to your Facebook Event Page, your blog post and any other websites that have information about the event. Use hashtags to better reach your audience ; hashtag the town that you're appearing in as well as #AuthorEvent. Tag the venue (if applicable) in your post too. You might get a re-tweet or two from that page, opening up the opportunity to reach more potential fans.

- Announce it on the home page of your website. Be sure to include all relavent information.

# 7: How much money should you spend on your book signing?

Again, this is entirely up to you but my suggestion is, as little as possible. This is where you the author---and this is probably the most important lesson in this book, need to wear your business person hat before committing to costly author events. As previously outlined, there are a variety of venues to hold your book signings but each one is going to vary significantly in cost. You need to give serious consideration on the matter of:

- Amount of books you'll need to sell to cover the cost of your table.
- Distance from your home to the venue.
- Cost of Lodging if overnight stays are necessary.

- Cost of fuel, food and marketing material for the event.

Let's assume that you're attending an author expo held at a public library and the event is free for authors to participate. This is great because so far you're not on the hook---you don't have to pay the library for use of their table. Let's also assume that the library is located in your hometown and you don't have to drive more than five miles to get there. This is also something that works in your favor. What also might work in your favor is the fact that since you're a local author in that community, you're more than likely to sell a decent amount of books at that particular event. Let's assume you've sold five copies of your book for $15.00 a copy. That's $75.00 in your pocket without breaking much of a sweat. Since you're not spending money on gas and lodging, you're ahead of the game with a decent profit.

Now, let's discuss some events that charge a modest amount of money to rent a table. There are author events that may charge anywhere from $25.00 to $80.00. This is still relatively inexpensive and if you can manage to sell five copies of your book at these events, you'll still turn a profit. However, let's assume you paid $50.00 to participate in the event and you've sold $75.00 worth of your books. That's a $25.00 profit, which is still very nice. Ask yourself this, though; how far away was the venue? How much did you spend on gas? How much did you spend on food? You may see that $75.00 disappearing very quickly and in the end, you've simply spent $50.00 to $75.00 on the privilege to appear at an author expo.

Okay, now let's talk about events that charge a hefty fee to rent space to sell your books. Comic Cons, and the like, charge a significant amount of money to rent table space---primarily due to the fact that these events are typically two to three days long. On average, Comic Cons charge artists, anywhere from $150.00 to $400.00 per event. The lower priced events are more or less new Comic Cons starting out with the hopes of growing into a larger-scale event. The higher-priced events are Comic Cons that are located in a large city catering to a huge market which draws a large audience throughout the two to three day run. Let's just assume that you're planning to rent a table that costs $150.00 at an event which runs from Saturday to Sunday and both days have a 10:00am-6:00pm event time.

Let's also assume for the sake of argument that you'll order twenty copies of your book specifically for the event. If you publish your books via CreateSpace, you as the author are purchasing copies of your own book at a large discount, not available to the general public. If the price you pay per discounted book is $3.25 and you order twenty copies, you'll pay CreateSpace $65.00. Of course, additional fees will be tacked on to that shipment of books. You'll pay tax and shipping and handling costs. Depending on where in the United States your order will be shipped to, this price will vary slightly. Conservatively let's just say that your total order costs $80.00 give or take a few dollars. Your $80.00 investment on a fresh stock of books plus the $150.00 table fee at the event has now set you back $230.00 and there are still a few more things to consider.

- How far away is the event from your home?
- How much fuel will your car consume driving to and from the event?
- Will you need to rent a hotel room for Saturday Night?
- How much will you need to spend on meals?

- Are you taking time off from your job to appear at the event?
- Will you feel comfortable inviting your fan base to see you at the event, knowing they will need to pay about $25.00 each for admission?
- How many copies of your book will you need to sell to at least break even?
- How many copies of your book will you need to sell to make a profit worth your time (8 hours each day plus travel) and energy?
- Are you confident that you can sell that many books?

Depending on the type of vehicle you drive, if the event is more than twenty five miles away, your fuel gauge will definitely reflect that. On the low side, let's assume that you're only using $10.00 worth of fuel for this event, it's now costing you $240.00 and you still need to think about lodging if your event if too far of a distance to drive back and forth from the event to your home and back and forth again the next day. If so, the upside is that events such as comic cons offer a discount deal with neighboring hotels if you're a vender at their event. Again, depending on where you're located and how pricy hotels are in that area, you'll need to think long and hard about whether or not it's worth the added cost. Conservatively, let's say that you'll spend Saturday night into Sunday at a hotel near your event for $80.00 a night. You're now paying $320.00. Another thing to keep in mind is that you're going to get hungry, both during and after the event. You can pack all the snacks you want to get you through the day, but after eight hours behind your table, continuously standing up and sitting down, talking to interested buyers, and people watching all day long, you're most definitely going to want to treat yourself to a sit-down meal after a long day. Whether that meal is eaten at McDonalds or The Capital Grille is entirely up to you, but let's low-ball and assume that you'll spend $20.00 on your meal (assuming that you're dining alone.) You're now spending $340.00 and you have only two days to make this amount back in book sales.

As discussed above, the twenty copies of your book that you've ordered for the event at a cost of $80.00 will need to be the star of the show. It will be up to you to turn those copies into pure profit, but at what cost? Well, at previous events such as the free library author expo, you sold your books at $15.00 each, so let's assume you'll do the same at a comic con. Let's say that you're an absolute bookselling pro and you've sold out of your twenty copies by the end of Sunday night. You'll have earned yourself $300.00---quite impressive. But wait one second; you'll still be $40.00 in the hole. I guess the best remedy for this is to try charging $20.00 per book. That will leave you with a gross of $400.00 and a profit of $60.00---for two long days of work on a weekend.

Oops, and I almost forgot to mention that you'll more than likely need to pay taxes on your sales for that event. Depending on what state your event is held, you're more than likely going to have a tax I.D in order to sell goods at that event. Rhode Island, for example, had implemented stringent tax laws and I.R.S. agents were visible throughout public events such as comic cons. On a positive note, Rhode Island has recently passed a bill which permits the sale of original and limited edition works of art exempt from state tax. Rhode Island was the first state to sign this bill into law and many other states will soon follow suit I'm sure. Be sure to check your local tax laws before selling your goods at events.

While I don't want to come off as pessimistic, I feel it's only fair for me to lay out every possible outcome, be it positive or negative. After all, book selling is a business whether or not the actual writing of your book was born entirely out of love and passion. In the end, you'll want to get your book in people's hands, but it shouldn't be at the cost of your own wallet. Sadly, I know some authors who spend a great deal of their time and money on book promotion events, yet their personal lives and, unfortunately, their finances suffer as a result of their shortsightedness. The practice of book selling really does need to be approached as a business. It can't be all fun and games.

# 8: Managing your expectations

It's important to manage your expectations when it comes to bookselling and hopefully I can shed a little bit of light on a few topics. The one thing to keep in mind is that more than likely you're not going to be an overnight success---bookselling is a tough business, especially when you're an unknown author. You need to prepare yourself for the long-haul and the fact that every person that approaches your table will not always walk away with one of your books.

As authors, we need to be honest with ourselves; people don't *need* our books---they aren't a necessity in people's lives, no matter how much we think they should be. We aren't at a table selling items that will make housecleaning simpler, cooking dinner easier or mowing a lawn faster. We aren't selling energy saving light bulbs, document shredders, smart phone chargers or any other items of importance that people use on an everyday basis. We're essentially selling items that people only care about after all of their responsibilities have been met. Sadly, the books that they do read are usually by well-known authors; hardly ever by unknown self-published authors.

There's a plethora of self-published authors out there, as I'm sure you're well-aware. What you may not be aware of is that according to Bowker's latest report (September 7, 2016), there have been more than 700,000 self-published books produced; that's a huge number of authors to compete with for a reader's attention. That's in addition to the already available 13 million books previously published by self-published authors.

The genre that your book falls into is also a determining factor in your selling success. Currently the Young Adult (YA), Romance and Mystery genre sees the best sales in the United States. Fantasy, Science Fiction and Horror---with the exception of high-caliber authors such as Stephen King, don't particularly see the same level of sales that the aforementioned do. If you're set up to sell and sign your books at bookstores, libraries, craft fairs or author expos, chances are that your YA, Romance or Mystery title will appeal to that particular audience. Science Fiction, Fantasy and Horror---your book might benefit greater by appearing at Comic Cons, Horror Expos and Speculative Fiction Conventions.

# 9: Speaking to your future fans

It's important to remember that unlike established and well-known authors who hold book signings---the ones with fans who have most likely already read their book(s) and are there specifically to meet said author, lesser-known authors who are independently published and are holding their signings in more unconventional settings will have much different encounters and interactions with folks who approach their table. Without coming off too negatively, people most likely aren't going to run up to your table and say things like, "Oh my God, I've read all of your books; I'm such a fan; it's an honor to meet you!"

What's more likely to happen is someone will timidly browse your book or books displayed on the table-

--perhaps just acting interested to humor you for a few seconds, but more often than not, they are mildly curious and could be teetering on the possibility of purchasing your book. This is where you need to be on your game and have your elevator pitch queued up---an engaging and gripping synopsis of the book they are glancing at or holding in their hands. Get that person interested in what you write, but do it without a high-pressure salesperson pitch. People don't like to feel pressured into things; it's why people don't like to stop at tables or even make eye contact with people---being put on the spot is never fun, I say this from personal experience. Keep the conversation casual and relaxed. If after you've described your book's topic and the person doesn't seem interested and is about to walk away, let them. Say thank you for stopping by and wish them a nice day. Sometimes people just don’t want to spend money on things and no amount of prodding is going to change that.

If, however, you’ve managed to grab their interest, discuss the book a little bit further. Tell them why you chose that particular topic or genre and ask questions such as who their favorite authors are or what genres they enjoy. Create a dialogue with them; this invokes a more relaxing exchange and as a result, a barrier is broken down between the author and the reader. This greatly increases your chance at book sales. Regardless of whether or not someone purchases your book, always smile, be courteous and say thank you for stopping by.

In addition to people who attend the events where you're selling your book---the people who attend with the intention of spending money, oftentimes there are people who attend events simply because it's free admission and they show up to kill some time. I've personally sat in on author panels at public libraries where the format was outlined for the authors to speak to the attendees in a Q and A styled forum and afterwards, the authors go to their book displays and await the people in attendance to visit their tables. Ninety percent of the audience left the room immediately after the Q and A without an ounce of interest in what the author's were trying to sell.

It wouldn't be so infuriating if the events weren't advertised as a "Support Local and Independent Authors" event.

Sometimes, you'll have a person approach you---someone who has no intention of buying your book, but instead is on a fact finding mission about how to publish their book that they've been working on for years. This is a bit of a slippery slope and should be handled very delicately. Obviously, you as an author know just how tedious and time consuming is can be to write a book, so you can certainly empathize. Conversations such as this, however, cannot become a detriment to your task at hand, which is to sell books. On occasion, I've been locked into a conversation with an aspiring author who had an abundance of questions on the publishing process---sometimes they've even tried pitching their book to me for publishing consideration, and I'd answered their questions to the best of my ability, but it does get to the point where you need to pull the plug and refocus your efforts on book buying customers. When you're trapped in an ongoing conversation and out of the corner of your eye you see someone peeking at your books, you need to excuse yourself so you can greet other people approaching your table. If you don't, you'll potentially lose sales. Be polite, be helpful, but don't be afraid to wrap up the conversation and wish them luck in their publishing quest.

# 10: Signing your books

Different authors have their own style of signings books but I'll offer my suggestion on signing your name on your books. First, make sure you have a nice legible signature. If penmanship wasn't your strong suit in grammar school, this is the time to reacquaint yourself with the art of the written word. Your book buying public won't be impressed with a messy, illegible scribble on a book that they spent their money on. Write your name largely enough that it's the focal point of the title page. It doesn't have to be John Hancock sized but scale it properly within the contrast of the size of the page. Cross out your printed name and sign your name underneath; this breaks down the barrier between the author and fan, thus creating a less formal relationship between the two and offers a more personal experience for the reader.

Optional, yet recommended is dating your signature at the upper right side of the title page. Let's say that your book signing is in Marshfield, Massachusetts on a beautiful July afternoon; you'd print *July 20, 2018* and directly underneath, print *Marshfield, MA* to identify the date and place of that particular signing.

You'll want to ask the buyer if they'd like their book personalized. Most times they will say yes and tell you to make it out to them or to someone that they intend to give the book to as a gift. Always double check the spelling of the name you're making the book out to. Names such as Mary or Joey are easy enough, but sometimes names such as Kaylee might be spelled Kayleigh and Devon could be spelled Devyn. Take an extra second to get the correct spelling.

Finally, be sure that you have space in front of you at your table to place the book firmly down in front of you to sign it neatly. There have been times where I've done group author events and the table was so cluttered that I'd needed to sign books standing up with the book in one hand as I signed it with the other. My signature looked like something I'd scribbled on a grocery list. Be sure that you have enough room at your table to prevent this.

# 11: Stay for the entirety of the event

Never leave an event early; it's unprofessional and you could lose out on potential sales. I've attended many events and witnessed a lot of authors pack up their booths early because of a lack of patrons throughout the day.

I myself am guilty of leaving an event early once---I brought along a friend who didn't turn out to be a good fit for an afternoon of book signing, and ultimately, my poor decision of leaving early cost me a book sale. I know because the person who showed up specifically for me told me later on how disappointed they were that I wasn't there. I've made certain to never let this happen again. We're professional authors and it's important that we act as such. The reputation that you develop throughout your career will be a key element in your overall success. One of the things that you'll be remembered by is how your conduct yourself at events that you attend.

Another good reason to remain at your event for the duration---be it a craft fair, author expo, comic con, is that other venders at the event could possibly stop by your booth to purchase something. After all, they've been stuck behind their own table for the majority of the event and might wander off to neighboring tables during the final thirty minutes of the event before other tables break their displays down. Be sure to meet and say hello to as many venders as you can throughout the event. Compliment the items that they are selling and make it know that you are an author selling books; invite them to visit your table when they have a chance. Every friendly exchange increases your chance at sales and future relationships with like-minded individuals.

# 12: If you are having bad sales at events; look at the solution, not the problem

If over time, you are continually having poor book sales, you're going to need to take a hard look at what you're doing wrong. As I mentioned before, you'll have good sales days and bad ones, but if you consistently have bad sales days, it's time to change course and do something differently. Observe what your peers are doing, especially the ones who seem to sell a steady volume of books at the same events that you're selling at. Keep in mind that it doesn't need to be another author; watch how the handmade jewelry makers entice passersby at craft fairs, how homemade preserves sellers attract their customers at the outdoor festivals, how DVD dealers display their products at horror conventions, so on and so forth. Implement their sure-fire methods into your routine.

Just because everyone's products for sale may differ, the objective is the same; to sell them to customers. Observe their delivery to people passing by their tables, how they set their displays up and present their products, their pitch, their personality. You can very well implement the routine that a successful homemade birdhouse vender uses into your own sales efforts. Learn from others, take mental notes, work their winning strategy into your own repertoire and move forward. Once you find your way into a winning sales strategy of your own, seize it and build upon it. Stay focused and be passionate. Build momentum, trust your instincts and always believe in yourself. With dedication, you will always get better and better.

# 13: Things you should do following your book signing

**Organize your contacts**

You're going to want to sort out the business cards that you collect throughout the event; contacts from fellow authors, editors, cover artists, bookstore managers, publishers---store these in a safe place for future reference. The various industry types that you'll meet will vary from event to event. You'll meet more cover artists and illustrators at comic cons, bookstore managers and industry elites at bookstores, and editors, agents, and---you guessed it, fellow authors at author expos.

Add their contact info to your preferred devices, look up their social media destinations and follow them. Send them a message within a day or two following the event to say how nice it was meeting them and you hope to see them at a future event in the near future. These small, yet friendly gestures go a long way with people, and the ones who appreciate it the most are the ones who will prove to be valuable contacts within your professional network.

**Share a brief rundown of your event on social media**

It's a good idea to post a short glimpse of your event on your social media outlets such as **Facebook**, **Twitter** and **Instagram**. Obviously your Twitter post will need to be brief as your posts are limited to (as of 2018) 208 characters. A photo from the event, a thank you to the venue who hosted the event and a hashtag in reference to your promotional efforts will suffice.

Do the same thing on Instagram; post your photo, a short description and your hashtags. You can post up to thirty hashtags in each post. Some popular hashtags to always include in your author-related posts are: **#booksigning #booksigningevent #booksigningtour #authorevent #writersofinstagram #authorsofinstagram #writersnetwork #readersofinstagram #bookrecommendations**

As far as Facebook; I find that things get a bit excessive and intemperate when authors share their thoughts about their events (and other topics) in their news feed. Keep it simple and remember that less is more. You don't need to write a novelette just because Facebook allows you to do so.

You should, however, post the best photos captured from the event and keep those limited to no more than six. Again, less is more. Most people don't like their news feed flooded with tons of images that they're expected to sift through.

**In summation**.

When all is said and done, there is no exact science to doing successful book signings. The main idea is to go out there, have fun and hopefully create a new fan base little by little. It takes a lot of time and devotion and only you can make your career as a writer happen. Over time, you'll find your niche and know what works best. You'll have ups, you'll have downs. Book signing success shouldn't only be measured in sales, but in how you build your professional character out there in the public, and by how many positive people you can meet and add to your professional network. And trust me when I tell you, there are so many amazing people out there to meet along the way. So get out there, enjoy yourself, sell your books and start building your fan base!

## About the Author

Rob Watts is an award-winning writer of fiction. He is the author of one novel, a short story collection, four novellas, and various inclusions in anthology releases. As an author, he has over one-hundred book signings under his belt since 2011 and continues to discover new and unconventional methods to promote his books. He currently lives in Boston.

**RobWattsOnline.com**

Also Available:

The Crooked Roads through Cedar Grove (2015)

Charms: Four Stories of Female Revenge (2017)

51325719R00077

Made in the USA
Middletown, DE
01 July 2019